BEES &POETRY

Compiled by

BRAD R. COOK

BEES & POETRY
Brad R. Cook

Published in the United States of America
by Broadsword Books LLC

isbn: 979-8-9865019-9-4
ebook isbn: 979-8-9865019-8-7

www.bradrcook.com

All pictures taken by Brad Cook
Honeycomb and black and white bee images from pixabay.com
Color bee image made by Brad Cook
Cover and interior designed by Brad Cook

For

Amber
& those who call our garden home

Save the Bees!
There are many ways to help bees
Plant a bee-friendly garden & protect bee habitats
Be a beekeeper, start or adopt a hive
Donate to organizations that help bees

Bees are an important part of our ecosystem

a bee
Matsuo Basho
(1644-1694)

a bee
staggers out
of the peony

Bumble Bee & Agastache | 2

3 | Bumble Bee & Bee Balm

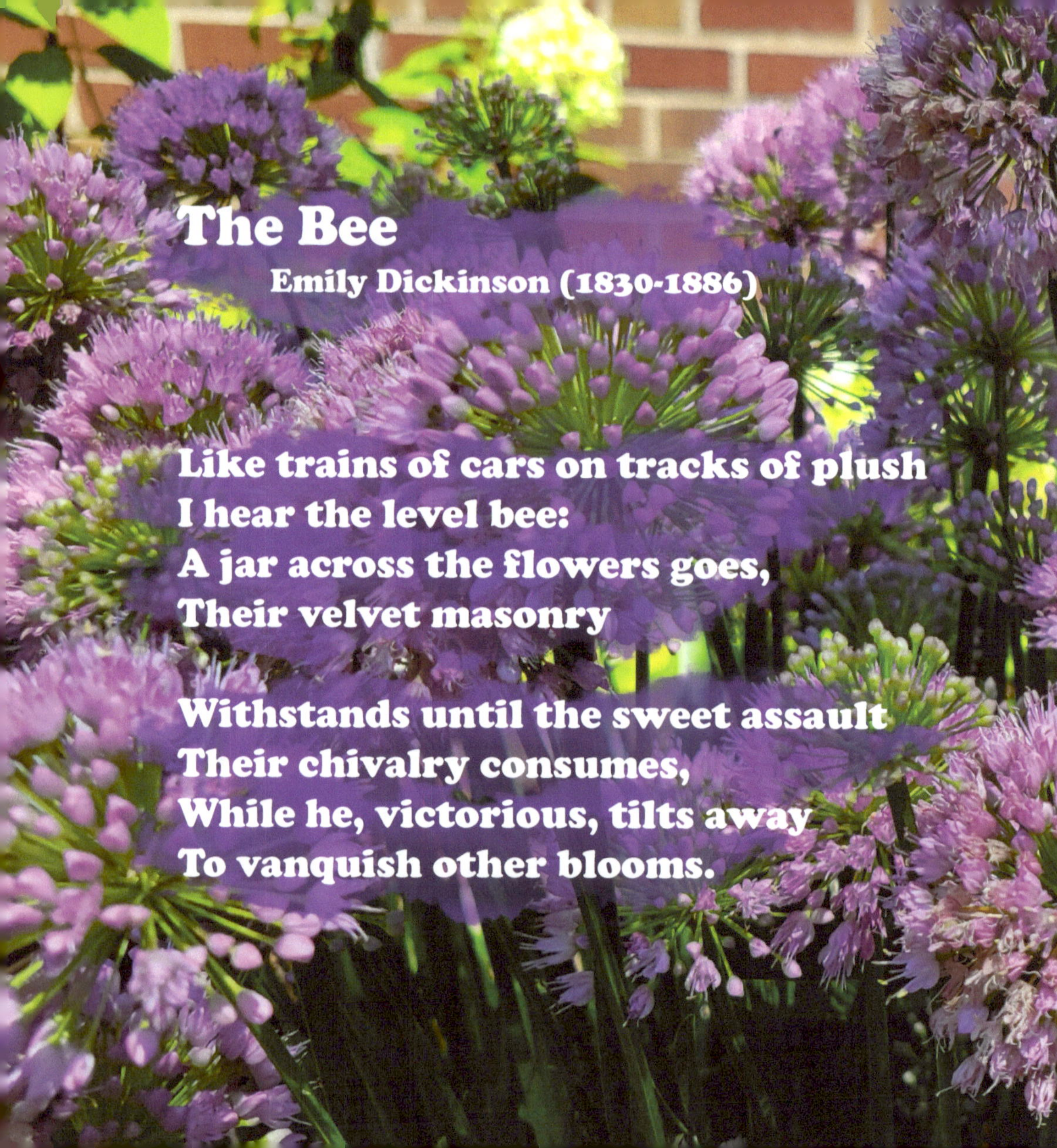

The Bee

Emily Dickinson (1830-1886)

Like trains of cars on tracks of plush
I hear the level bee:
A jar across the flowers goes,
Their velvet masonry

Withstands until the sweet assault
Their chivalry consumes,
While he, victorious, tilts away
To vanquish other blooms.

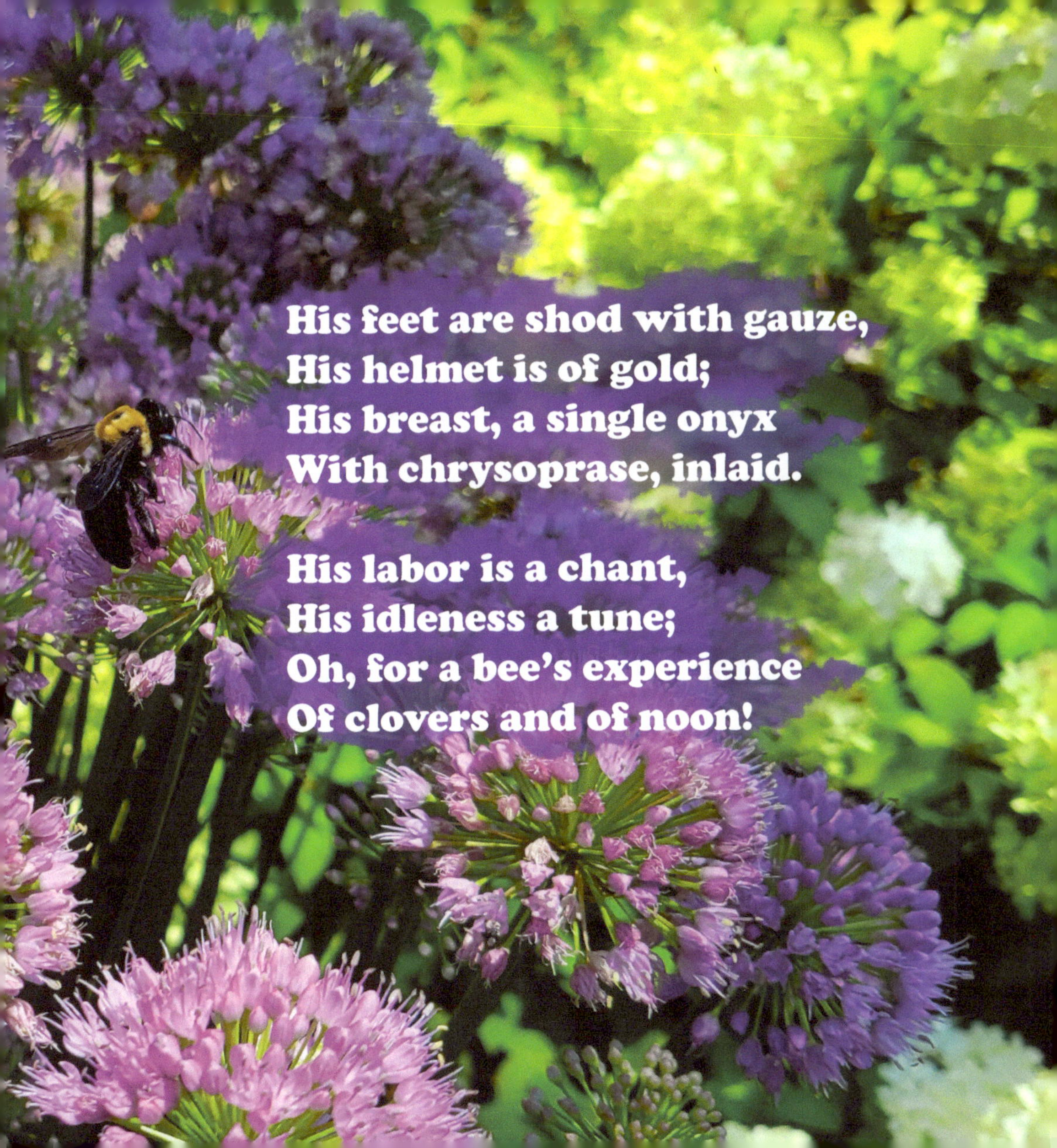

His feet are shod with gauze,
His helmet is of gold;
His breast, a single onyx
With chrysoprase, inlaid.

His labor is a chant,
His idleness a tune;
Oh, for a bee's experience
Of clovers and of noon!

Bumble Bee & Hydranga

Save the Bees!

Brad R. Cook

Save the bees!
Save the pollinators!
Save the world!

I do not jest
the mighty bee is best
at averting this planet's regress.

Save the bees!
Save the pollinators!
Save the world!

Nature's stinger
Pollen bringer
and stamen ringer

Save the bees!
Save the pollinators!
Save the world!

Trying to be discrete
Searching a world of concrete
Until their quest is complete.

Save the bees!
Save the pollinators!
Save the world!

Honey Bee &
Ornimental Onion

The Lake Isle of Innisfree
W. B. Yeats (1888)

I will arise and go now, and go to Innisfree,
And a small cabin build there, of clay and wattles made:
Nine bean-rows will I have there, a hive for the honey-bee;
And live alone in the bee-loud glade.

And I shall have some peace there, for peace comes dropping slow,
Dropping from the veils of the morning to where the cricket sings;
There midnight's all a glimmer, and noon a purple glow,
And evening full of the linnet's wings.

I will arise and go now, for always night and day
I hear lake water lapping with low sounds by the shore;
While I stand on the roadway, or on the pavements grey,
I hear it in the deep heart's core.

Bumble Bee & Magnolia

Honey

Brad R. Cook

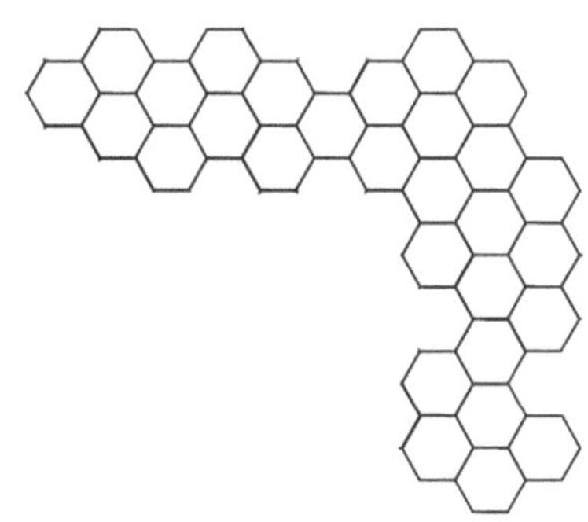

Golden nectar on
Warm bread with melted butter
Intoxicating

Honey Bee & Allium Millenium

The Humble Bee
Ralph Waldo Emerson (1837)

Burly dozing humblebee!
Where thou art is clime for me.
Let them sail for Porto Rique,
Far-off heats through seas to seek,
I will follow thee alone,
Thou animated torrid zone!
Zig-zag steerer, desert-cheerer,
Let me chase thy waving lines,
Keep me nearer, me thy hearer,
Singing over shrubs and vines.
Insect lover of the sun,
Joy of thy dominion!
Sailor of the atmosphere;
Swimmer through the waves of air,
Voyager of light and noon;
Epicurean of June,
Wait, I prithee, till I come
Within ear-shot of thy hum,—
All without is martyrdom.
When the south wind, in May days,

With a net of shining haze,
Silvers the horizon wall,
And, with softness touching all,
Tints the human countenance
With a color of romance,
And, infusing subtle heats,
Turns the sod to violets,
Thou, in sunny solitudes,
Rover of the underwoods,
The green silence dost displace,
With thy mellow breezy bass.

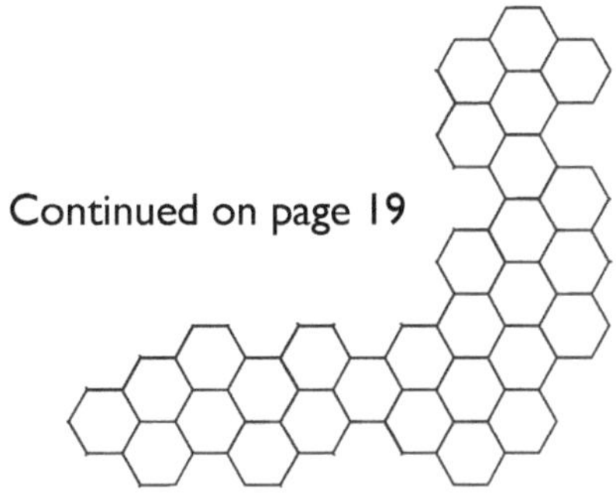

Continued on page 19

15

Honey Bee & Yarrow

Hot midsummer's petted crone,
Sweet to me thy drowsy tune,
Telling of countless sunny hours,
Long days, and solid banks of flowers;
Of gulfs of sweetness without bound
In Indian wildernesses found;
Of Syrian peace, immortal leisure,
Firmest cheer, and bird-like pleasure.
Aught unsavory or unclean,
Hath my insect never seen;
But violets and bilberry bells,
Maple-sap and daffodels,
Grass with green flag half-mast high,
Succory to match the sky,
Columbine with horn of honey,
Scented fern, and agrimony,
Clover, catch fly, adder's-tongue,
And brier-roses, dwelt among;
All beside was unknown waste,
All was picture as he passed.
Wiser far than human seer,
Yellow-breeched philosopher!
Seeing only what is fair,
Sipping only what is sweet,
Thou dost mock at fate and care,

The Humble Bee by
Ralph Waldo Emerson
(Continued)

Leave the chaff and take the wheat,
When the fierce north-western blast
Cools sea and land so far and fast,
Thou already slumberest deep;
Woe and want thou canst out-sleep;
Want and woe which torture us,
Thy sleep makes ridiculous.

Ode to the Lone Bee
Brad R. Cook

Hello, lone bee.
On the way to your colony?

Legs covered all in,
Colorful particles of pollen.

Honey maker,
Golden nectar baker.

Living the high life,
In a hive without strife.

The queen doth command,
That the bee make it grand.

A hexagon creator,
and garden pollinator.

Beware their stinger,
The pain, even death, bringer.

But know they are humble,
Just a drone looking to bumble.

Tucked up in a petal's flap,
Resting for a little nap.

For the bee, nature's caretaker,
Spreads flowers over every acre.

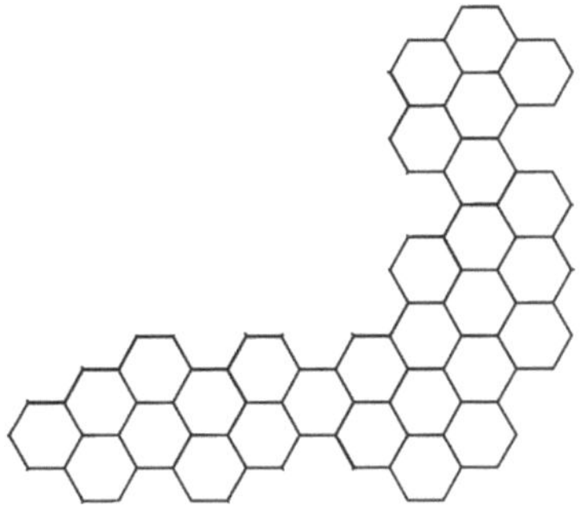

Honey Bee & Friends

Fame is a Bee.

Emily Dickinson (1861)

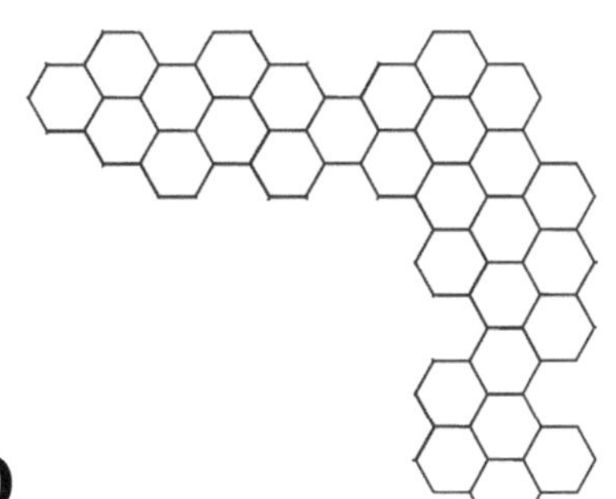

Fame is a bee.
It has a song—
It has a sting—
Ah, too, it has a wing.

Find the Bees

Butterfly

*Find the Bees - there are 5 bees.

Cicada

More Bugs In My Garden

Birds, rabbits, ants, butterflies, crickets, cicadas, lady bugs, beetles, a cat, a squirrel, and several types of bees call my garden home.

Butterfly

Lady Bug

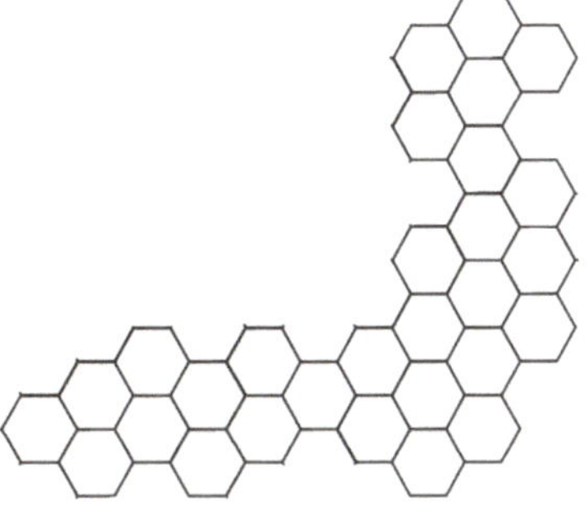

Acknowledgments

Thank you to my wife, Amber who worked on this garden oasis with me. It's a glorious garden. Most of the photographs were taken in our garden over three seasons.

A thank you to the bees. I can't imagine a world without your buzzing, without your flowers, and without your meandering flights. Bees are amazing and a bit mischievous, but there is nothing quite as adorable as a bee taking a nap in a flower.

Thank you for caring about bees!
Save the bee, save the world.
Please keep advocating for bees, and maybe plant a flower or two for them.

Be calm around bees and bees will be calm around you.

Books by Brad R. Cook
The Iron Chronicles: Iron Horsemen | Iron Zulu | Iron Lotus
The Airdrainium Adventures: Steamtree | Geartree | Stonetree
The History of St. Louis Writers Guild: Celebrating a Century
The Remarkable Journey of the First Road Trip Across America
Numerous Short Stories
Anthologies: Weird STL | Where Rivers Meet | Love Letters to St. Louis

About the Author

Brad R. Cook
Author & Historian

I see things that never were and say, "Why not?"

Brad R. Cook is the author of nine novels, twelve short stories, and has been included in eight anthologies. When not outlining his next fantasy adventure, he can be found researching odd moments for another historical fiction, or sharing people's stories with his non-fiction. He began as a playwright, dipped into the corporate writing world, and served as co-publisher and acquisitions editor for Blank Slate Press. For over seventeen years, he has served as a board member of St. Louis Writers Guild, including three and a half years as president. Dedicated to helping his fellow writers, he has coordinated and planned over forty book fairs, writers' conferences, and conventions. In 2016, he formed Broadsword Books LLC to publish his own work and help other authors with book covers, ebooks, print book interiors, and promotional materials. He learned to fence at thirteen and never set down his sword, but prefers to curl up with a centuries-old classic.

@bradrcook on Bluesky, Threads, Instagram, Facebook, and Tumblr
Plus, book themed t-shirts and other apparel at
BroadswordBooks on RedBubble.com

bradrcook.com

www.ingramcontent.com/pod-product-compliance
Lightning Source LLC
Chambersburg PA
CBHW041626110726
48005CB00002B/509